Con Todo

By:
Geniece Trevino

Copyright © 2021 Birdcage Ink

All rights reserved. No part of this book may be reproduced, distributed, or transmitted in any form or by any means, including photocopying, recording, or other electronic or mechanical methods, without the prior written permission of the publisher, except in the case of brief quotations embodied in reviews and certain other non-commercial uses permitted by copyright law.

First Paperback Edition Aug 2021

ISBN: 978-0-578-83609-6 (paperback)

Published by Birdcage Ink
www.Birdcageink.com

Cover Art by
www.Ebonydesignedit.com

To: My boys
For with wide eyes and childlike belief in my dreams you made me certain they would come true.

To: Lorenza my Abuelita
For without your faith, encouragement, and utmost belief in me I would've most certainly given up

To everyone that was reader of my jumble before this publication:
Without you guys this book would still be scattered amongst composition books and crumbs of paper.

Dear Readers,

When I was younger I grew up alongside my sister and my two other cousins. We spent most of our time with our abuela and most of summers at her kitchen counter. Stories, dramas, family novelas it all happened there in that kitchen. The kitchen counter was our family gathering place. We'd tell her our secrets, she'd make tortillas, we'd do our homework, we celebrated birthdays, and we ate great food. My grandmother is an amazing cook. We joke that the reason we spend so much time at the counter and in the kitchen, is because we're always eating. Which wouldn't be a lie. My grandmother would cook everything, but nothing was like her bean & cheese burritos when we were younger. As we got older she would serve us everything. I could come over with the worst problems and plop myself down at her counter in tears and she would say, "Quires comer mija?" I would spill out my tribulations while she bustled around the kitchen making a plate. She'd put it down and say "con todo" in a ta-da way that only she can do. "With everything," she would repeat in English, we would eat and talk about life and the universe and the chisme.

On my plate of life ...

Con todo,

NieceBird

No llores

When I was a little girl
and my parents would argue
the world seemed rough
I would cry on the cold countertop
my grandmother would rub my back and say,
 "No llores mija confía en el señor."

I am in my twenty's
A mother
A student of life experiences
I wallow in my shallow pools of love
I cry to her
"el no entiende nada"
"No llores mija," she squeezes my shoulder
"don't you have faith you will be ok?"

It's 2am and I thought I had found the love of my life
Father of my sun, yet we orbit different paths
Collision

It's 2 am and all I could think about was my grandmother
Telling us little girls if we ever wake up around this time
And feel down to kneel down and say a prayer

I close my eyes
T E A R S
No llores mija I whisper to my heart

Decoration

"But it's all so objective," I whined, "nothing more than decoration."

"Decoration?" she asked with a puzzled look smeared across her face.

"Decoration" I repeated, "and I'm nothing more than wallpaper."

I watched as she pondered my answer without the slightest clue what I was talking about. Confident I'd lost her in my maze of vagueness I began to change subjects, but …

"I'm not sure I understand," she urged "wallpaper...how so?"

I snickered as if this concept were common knowledge to just anyone.

"If your everyday interactions or relationships with people were …" I stopped suddenly realizing how rusty it all sounded out loud.

"Were," I continued to expel the dusty theory. "Were… viewed as objects in your house…who would be the first to welcome you home after a long day regardless of good or bad, only to be pushed aside in seconds. You know this person. We all have them, we just don't refer to them as our front door." I paused for a minute admiring the insanity, "Then you head to your fridge, this cold box that stores vital nutrients necessary to help sustain your everyday life. You take what you need and let's be honest no one tells their fridge 'thank-you'. You see where I'm going with this…?" I grinned.

MCT--[20130813]

When I think back on her and the world she sheltered me in, I realize she never hid me on earth. The concept seems rash to those who don't think to understand & for the longest time--I didn't. The mind is capable of unlimited possibilities if you're brave enough to get devoured by the dimensions of consciousness. Most of us aren't. Fearing we'll come across the unseen voice embedded deep in the mind of all earthlings.

Once you realize the voice was your own all along, fear fades into nothing more than playful gestures. After you overcome the fear of yourself, thoughts become answers not choices. You drift from being the question to the most blatant answer. Confidence is not obvious, it will not walk up and shake your hand. It will not grow stronger through compliments or happy thoughts. No confidence my dear does not have a pretty face. It's hideous and hides itself from any sign of danger. It lurks somewhere between nightmares & self-doubt. Deeply entangled in all your fears, becoming a fear in itself. Because if you weren't afraid of yourself, then what would be left to fear but fear itself?

The thought alone scares you

Wrap your head around ideals.
Master your heart
F
  A
    L
      L
Out of place
S p r e a d your seeds of creativity
Open your hands to inspiration
Give with spirit
Take with a humble heart
Grow like the seeds of our mothers

PARASITE.

There was the vague concept of thought, of course, and how much of my time it took up.
Living in my mind like a parasite. It continues to chew away at the outer layer of brain.
Another piece of myself digested into the lowest form of filth,
which of course lies in the hallows of my head.
Wasting precious thoughts on unreachable souls.
My essence will never hibernate in the mind I crave.
The thoughts chew through the first layer as I sit there motionless, oblivious to my surroundings.
Just me vs my thoughts. like a parasite living rent free in my cage.
I want to infect someone, to become a piece of them.
Float through their veins, filling their body, past the pumping heart, I'll latch.
 Just for a glimpse.
I'll float on near the retina and enjoy your view,
but again, I'll float on.
My destination is the highest.
Ride the veracious veins to the brain.
Nestled right below the skull; I settle.
Grow my roots, but I'm no parasite.
I only wish you thought of me,
as I did you.

{21042014; 12:22p.m}

I wanted to hide amongst the fallen leaves and left behind nuisance.
Somewhere they told me I belonged.
There was an ease in embracing my surroundings for what they were.
A photosynthesis of life. To lack anything was simply misunderstanding.
No cause for tremble it's all right here, but your looking there
 & no one looks for a leaf in the middle of a forest.

They were constantly asking what I wanted.
What it was they were doing wrong,
I didn't feel what I wanted should have to be explained,
furthermore, I didn't know how to explain it.

I wanted to be rescued
not so much from this place
as much as I longed to be rescued from the burdens of my mind.
The torturous ridicule always stemmed from the shit I can't seem to forget.
Its haunting and I can't escape it.

The gaping hole pulling me closer each chance it gets.
They ask what I want as I stare at the dark black hole
I want the universe, not the whole universe of course,
just yours for a mere moment.

As artificial as it may sound
I long for the 'meaning'
I want to sleep in someone's brain till morning

Don't ask me what I want its far too complicated
I confide in Orion while he takes a shower
Staring at the stars I make it as simple as possible

I want to exist.
I long for someone to see for my full potential,
even when I, myself have lost sight of it.

Yet, my mind mocks this

for I need no one but myself
and I cuddle next to my brain for the night
as my loneliness consumes me.

Emerge

As dark and light collide
the stars welcome the night
inviting, enticing the foreign mystery of darkness

We lie awake,
rendering the silence
then nothing happens

The urge to explain
it eats them from the spine
words as fragile as knives

until you look
the starry night unraveling in your eyes
blanketing away the hopelessness

Struggling voiceless
words like a trap

we emerge

The Perks of an Insomniac

It's the early morning I spend awake pondering nonsense,
letting the gears in my mind move like clockwork,
trying to remember as much as I can
before the ocean of emotions and memories retreats once again.
It's in the middle of the night when inspiration strikes me deep in my core,
and I can't help but reach for the ink and paper.

I could sit there for hours
 just trying to conjure up the right word
 to describe the feeling of that exact moment.
It's when the whole world seems to be asleep
that I feel safest unfolding every dark corner
of my mind and bringing it to the light.

I can still feel you

& I sat there looking at the stars
longing for someone to talk to
searching my mind for the soul I wanted to confide in
only to realize the people I long for
only exist in the past.

In·er'tia (noun.)

The moment in your life you begin to question what exactly you are doing with your life. It's the moment you realize that fate is an illusion and it's time to dedicate your life to a conscious decision. Any decision. Instead of asking ourselves are we strong enough, deciding to be strong enough. Strong enough to shift the routine momentum we so often get ourselves into. Work, school, hustle, provide, but does it make us human? Then it hits you like a rushing river and you're left with the decision to shift momentum— you can swim or you can continue along the banks and remain unchanged. After all inertia is all about momentum.

Momentum \mō-'ment- əm, mə-'ment-\ *n, pl:*
1: the quantity of motion of a moving body, measured as a product of its mass and velocity.
2: the impetus gained by a moving object
3: It's like the feeling you get when the mundane cycles of life catch you. It's like your running down a hill & suddenly it hits you; you've been running down a hill at full speed, you're heading straight for the curb & you're running too fast to catch yourself. You either run straight into the fall or change direction, but the minute it hits you it's impossible to forget. You become aware of the momentum you harness. Your mass. Your density. The sheer velocity that got you caught up in this momentum to begin with.

"And that's all I am to you…a muse'" he muttered under his breath.
Far from I screamed inside.
These harsh illusions straying me from the page.
How dare I document you?
How dare I utter a word of how you crippled me
How despite our darkness we flourished?
Ushering in Motherhood like moss
we grew when watered

limiting yourself to a muse
amuse the writer,
to spite her,
despite her,
excite her

In the right situation, of course
light her fire
tell the writer in her

Prior, to all the bowls & laughter
Five years of trying to start a new chapter
"That's all I am to you a muse"
 As if I didn't sit here and chose
you
        &
                you
Through Boulders and the Blues
booze, bruises, and views
loose screws & untied shoes
It was always you

who's whose
M U S E
I listen as he screams a song
to pull us through this
taboo

[9:44:00P.M Pacific Standard Time 20182905]

COMA CLUSTER
[NGC-4882]

I am a blackhole.
An epitome of vast assumptions,
devouring curious souls, thriving in
shadows beneath scattered leaves from
distant dimensions I am unseen. Swallowing light
to cloak the seams of my existence. Frequencies as
wide as the ocean tug at the toes of optimistic
explorers. Sacrificing heart to drown in darkness
"Who can love a blackhole?" I echo through the
cosmos. I am nothing. Feasting on a plate of everything,
with no escape velocity. I engulf those within reach.
A stain on a blanket of stars. I am a blackhole. A
cloaked thought brewed in the relentless mind
of time. I go unseen. For I am nothing, you
see? Feasting on a plate of
EVERYTHING

The Language of Flowers

Time is not the mother of love
I write as my sun sleeps
his steady breathing
calming the waves of my soul
Moss covers my empty belly as I weep
I seemed to have lost one down the sink
of time lost
As I lie here covered in moss

Density

What if it was never about gravity
what if it's about density
Sheer Mass if you will
depth in souls
keeping us grounded
Who have we become besides the birds afraid to fly?

Atop the telephone poles we plot
our destination dependent upon a season

Mind over Matter
Mass in our Minds

keeping us
right
where
we
are

Motherhood

Sleepless nights & coffee survival
Taking a nerf bullet and escaping the store without a hot wheel
Taking pieces of me to build a better you
Braver
Stronger
Confident
Admiring the men you've become
Motherhood; an admiration of life
Creation at its most humble
For I am not fully me without a piece of you

We we're straddled in a desk chair when
he said he didn't think I'd come back
as if I'd ever truly left

He was inside of me
Yet, it wasn't about finishing
as we slowly rocked back and forth
We were just as close to the bottom as we were to the top
His glass infinitely full

That's how it went with us
there was just something about being inside
each other that mattered most.

Appreciation over possession
Bound by collision
We emerge
Our glass infinitely full
yet, we have no thirst

So, it is written so it shall be.

I will never scream I'm worth it to someone ever again.

Not with my voice.

Not with my body.

Not with spirit.

Worth is measured by belief

I believe in my voice

I believe in my body

I believe in my spirit

Acknowledge my own intentions

SOMEONE I LOVED ONCE TOLD ME

Someone I loved once told me
I didn't know how to love
That my frequency wasn't strong enough
That my appetite for action
Wouldn't keep me warm at night
That despite the persistence
I wasn't warm enough,
Brave enough,
Mindful enough.
That I didn't know how to love
My cooked meals and thirsty hips
Didn't claim your heart
My open arms didn't give you enough space
My spirit didn't ease your storm
Someone I loved once told me
I didn't know how to love…
You.

Note to self: One of us is missing

It's November
& I'm writing so you exist on paper
I'm writing because it's cold
& I'm your mother

It's November
& you're missing your special quilt nana had made
& for the life of me I'll never remember your name
or the shape of your face

The alchemist in me breathes you to life on paper
When I should be snuggling you to bed

But it's November and one of us is missing

ANIMAL

Perched below the hilltop
Buried in trees
We'd rise in smoke

The last bench on the far right
A rock disguised as a diamond
We both cherished

Grunge drummer
Broken arm by parked car
Didn't keep him from the sticks

We'd run as fast as a red mustang
With a puppet riding shotgun
I wish you could call me a liar

"Prosthetic," he'd say
While we perched on the bluffs
The nothing always made sense
Even if nothing made sense.

I told you so...

I felt like my mother
Eyes as dry as Death Valley by sunrise
The packed clothes in the car

Soothed by the mother before her
Crippled by the emotions
We dare not feel
For lovers
Who dare not heal

Skin like sandpaper grit
She hugs me regardless
And she'll never admit
I told you so

Love is not flat
Love is not always
Love is embracing the 'not always'

A heart has curves & abrupt stops
It's the decision to keep going
That make a heart what it is

The flow
The flow at the bumps in the road
The flow

Flow is what makes the pattern so easy it beats.

I stared at the stained porcelain rim
I couldn't swallow I couldn't even tell if I was breathing
My heart was so loud I began to cry. It was sharp.
I had been holding my breath.
The tile cold beneath my shaky hands.
I didn't want to look anymore, but I couldn't move
My eyelids stained in the deep red
I slammed the lid closed & sat on the seat
Silent sobs
I couldn't make a noise
I wanted to scream, to yell for help.
My heart spoke for my tongue with all the pounding
I caught my reflection in the mirror
And all I could say was sorry
Because I couldn't make a sound
Because I couldn't scream
Because I flushed the toilet
& see red in my dreams.

Everything Comes Next

I sat in bed
Cold milk in a mug with a spoon
Oreos beside me
I'm not where you left me
Cold

I ate my cookies with a spoon
I don't remember where Phil told us to hide our love
In the canyon saloon
Behind the moving staircase
Everything comes next
but I can't remember where it went

A quiet place
We hide within sight
Watching
Because everything comes next

Channel 11

He's just a fucking Sitcom
Tuesday & Wednesday
Nights after 11pm
Pacific Standard Time
His face shows up at the screen door
He shines in the limelight of the porch light
& for a second I think about changing the channel
But don't we all love a good sex scene

08082013 3:25pm Pacific Standard Time

But it made perfect sense, if nothing here was more than just unsaid truths waiting to leak from our lips in moments of too much intensity. God forbid anything here promote too much pain through honesty. Feelings were made to be hurt in more ways than one. In fact, I found that was one of the hardest concepts for these human's grasp, the uncertainty of emotions they themselves produce. I mean after all what are thoughts anyway if not the unsaid words left boiling in our head to stew until morning.

Critical relapses on my faceless journey
To an untamed eye the concept seems morbid
A scuff on polished veneer
Such a grand gesture as to not want one's face
Intentions were quite often questioned and
Nearly always predetermined
But honesty is always polar opposite & never dressed for the occasion
I wanted to be ripped from memory like the half-spoken pages of my notebook
Not a single word remembered not a single word forgotten.

Theoretically

Theoretically, he's just a bookseller
Prim & Proper
Except for the one stray hair on his beard
Grown to elude the image of being
Prim & Proper

Theoretically,
He's a cager
Though few know the meaning
Never late, Proper attire
Turkey sandwich

"Are you making a mess?" He asks with a chuckle
I box my rants and put them on a shelf in the back
Buried in books

Theoretically, I have fifteen minutes left
We knew a man once that had a pet octopus
Whose name we never knew

Theoretically,
I'm not even sure I know you,
But I am making a mess

Page 61

The two made signs of peace
agreed to travel together.
However,
satisfied of the treacherous intentions
that he himself grasped

At the same instant
Tempted their respective parts
Missed fire

Both exposed to the fire of the others
Whom lay upon the ground
Together underneath it all

Taking which followed them for some distance

But it was just like she told me it would be—Simple.
Understanding the simplicity is the miscommunication.
Brewing internal and external miscommunication in the same pot drowns the message.
It's as simple as you make it.

The compilation of ideas birthing permanent concepts of good and bad.
They breed within us reproducing the beautiful apparatus of doubt.
Coddled like a baby in our hearts we love what was never ours to begin with.
Fathering resistance within, we endure what we feel we deserve.
Sheltering the only child of choices from harms reach.
& we endure.

Fostering doubt for our peace of mind
Doubt knows not where it comes from
Nor does it ask questions or care
Doubt is thankful to be cared for and fed

&& in return, we endure
Thankful for the company within such a desolate place like the mind.

Pieces of What

Human withering was by far the worst display of self-sacrifice.

A flower may lose its color and become frail and weak

The withering of a human is much different you see,

for it loses not its color or strength.

No, its composure will not call for help

Instead it endures.

It reassures.

It believes in the odds

Which in turn is the morbid difference,

between the decay of a human to a flower.

Because even as a flower is dying it stains its petals in honesty.

Cause & Effect

It no longer served my happiness.
It wasn't lacking effort,
It was lacking purpose.
Cause & Effect

It's 1a.m
& the cycle of scribbling my troubled thoughts is back

Cause:
An empty bed speaks any tongue

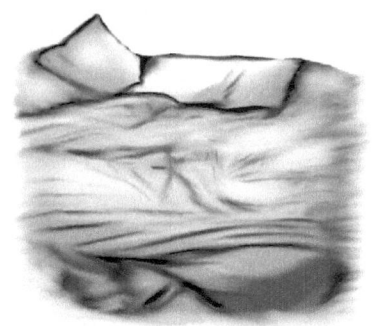

WHITNEY

Skin colored like the freshly turned dirt
Humble heart rough hands
Beneath the stars of Whitney

We sit in darkness
With the flicker of his cigarette
He points out the heroes hidden in the stars

He hides in plain sight
In rows of lettuce, corn, papas
Quiet as a field mouse
Strong like the horse
He places a tiny girl on the saddle

The girl teared up
"No hay nada que temer flaca"
He chuckles

She closes her eyes
Takes a deep breathe
"Aggarate tu mismo"
Hold onto yourself
He shouts as he hit the horse
With a swat that jolts
Her eyes open

She's 27
Skin like turned soil
Looking Orion square in the eye

I WILL NEVER BE THE LAKE

I always feel like the people I crave always want calmer waters.
It's like the lakes are more relaxing
and the ocean is always unpredictable.

The rivers sing pretty songs
and the waves of the ocean crash down.
You can lose yourself in the ocean,
but the shore is always visible on the lake.

I will never be the lake
and as much as that saddens me
I have to accept that that all of me
doesn't fit into a bowl carved into the earth.

I am dangerous.
I am curiosity.
I am depths with creatures that have yet to be found.
I am the horizon staring at its reflection.
Come swim in me.

THE WASHING OF THE FEET

Huddled together in the candlelight
The deep tones echoing off the stained glass
Collected energy

Deep hums of adoration
We walk together
Flooding love with every stride

The sunflower stands tall in her green dress
As she dips her roots in the water
A photosynthesis of love
Humbly kissed on her roots with honor

We walk together and apart

I thought I'd write about how you destroyed me
How the moon controlled calypso by pulling at her heart strings
But in that I'd have to admit to the floods and the hurricanes.

To drowning myself in darkness
A misinterpretation of the night

To a harboured fear of solitude
Embraced
Simply so you could enjoy low tide

KETTLE ON THE STOVE

Here's to book talks and raging arguments
Putting the kettle on the stove
Here's to empty bank accounts and full bowls
Here's to climbing mountains and digging holes
To sleepless nights & one bathroom
Here's to always finding our way back & stumbling our way forward
To unwatered ferns and winter harvests
Here's to Whitney Portal and Estes Red Rum
Here's to guiding a being through the wormhole
& watering the amazing person, he's bloomed into
To forgiveness & exposure
To long laughs & even longer cries
Here's to being just as close to the bottom as we are to the top.

WHO TOOK THE KETTLE OFF THE STOVE?

You let the water get cold
Our boiling passion is no longer whistling

Nuzzled in a blanket I wait for a miracle
Throat as dry as tea leaves
I choke on I miss you

Two hearts
One house
& we let the water get cold

BEE STINGS & BLACK SAND

All I see is rain & a drowned tent
24mi of everything I walked away from
Yet, the tide never reaches me
Even the highest tide never washes you from my beach

I drove 8hrs to the ocean & brought the desert with me
Scariest shit I ever had to do
What was supposed to teach me endurance
Only taught me silence & patience
There's no race to be run

Even the loneliest of lighthouses
Still welcomes you home
5mi in the dark
Racing the pull of the moon

I may have made it home
But I still never escaped you

Desperation

With small memories and large expectations
I want to hold you
The old you; Not you
But the time in which you existed

Time
The times I held my breath for love
Lines on line that we lined
to align

Desperation settles disagreements
Do not come to me in desperation
Do not come to me with future agreements

I want to hold you
No, not you
But the crumbs of you I followed to get
To me

All Honey No Milk

Hands as rough as
The life he leads
No complaints here
His heart won't allow it

All honey no milk
His sweet voice spills out thick
I spread it on my bad days

In a land of readers
With nothing read
Buried in books

We sit in silence
Louder than a sea of people
Drowning in smoke

Skin as dark as my heart
We worry not
To be seen
To be heard
To be felt

I look back at my shadow
But it stands beside me
All honey no milk
As I drown myself in smoke

Forgotten

Tightly rolled cigarettes
Burned into my ashtray of memories
If forgotten could speak
Would she whisper or scream?

Brushed under the rug of time
I linger with the dust
Pick me up like a penny
you don't want stuck

Stuck is the perfect adjective
if that even exists
Stuck like the last thought before bed
Fitting itself into your dreams
Tucked in neatly in the corner

Stuck
Stuck like a ring you weren't supposed to try on
Fitting as tight and uncomfortable as a
Long car ride with a stranger

If forgotten could speak
she would whisper
Whoever your trying to forget already forgot you
If forgotten could speak
you would scream
**Because those trying to forget don't want to be
Forgotten**

Annotated Bibliography

I gather my notes of absence
The when's and where's
Examples to prove my honesty

Hanging lines of history
To support our thesis

Gather all the notes,
Underlines,
And moments of importance

It's all there
In order
But you can't help but wonder

Am I formatting this right?

THE DADS

Its all just rivers & saloons
It makes us go the distance
Everything good comes in threes

Flights & Isabella Blondes
Form the bond

Speak with your hands
Not with your mouth
Show me you care

80 through the canyon
You didn't close your eyes
I'm afraid if I close mine

You'll slip away like a dream
Or the way the river rips through
The canyons seams

Bathroom wall

Why does it feel comfortable?
Because we are taught at an early age that its private
Because it hides our private parts
But does it hide our private parts

Our unfiltered singing voice
The sobs no one will ever hear
Missed periods, made periods,
Cries of punctuation

The shit we say to ourselves
When we stand on the other side
Of that mirror
Small hands under the door
Reaching for every shroud of attention
Such a small space for such depth
But I promise you
Once you notice it
The tile has never looked more comforting

Family resume

I could wash my hands in bleach
But the dirt of my previous life
Would linger under my nails

Five years of sobering my resume
And I can still feel the hesitancy
I cleansed my soul & drowned in
Normal

The luck of escaping I guess
I read between the lines
they'll never forget my nose crossed
Who am I?

A question I never had to ask
Books and obscure quotes
protecting my soul.
Validating the human I cling to

Thankful enough to know I didn't
lose myself between the lines
I only lost the you,
you thought you knew.

I've both loved & hated these prayers
that saved my heart
In whispers
In sobs and sighs
In the earliest of mornings
And the darkest of situations
Etched in my breath
As I forgive myself
For letting them trespass against me

LOVE CRIME JUNKIES

Link always finds Zelda
Over it, over again, and again
head Vs heart
war of Eternities

Can I keep you?
pRess play on the podcast
roll me In white grape
My face on your shoulder at
Emo night

don't be afraid to Jump
oUr life
closed captioNed
Kinda messy
Isn't it
dEspite everything you
Stay keeping me up

He hugs me like sandpaper
My skin stained brown like the wood
he carves; leaving his mark

I sit stretched out like a cat
In the sunlight
In the room with all the windows
we're too afraid to look out of

If you found your reflection
walking down the street
Would you even say hello?

If you found your reflection
in another person
Would you be confident
you know what love is?

A ring of emptiness. It surrounds the mind. A pit of black -- leaves room for inspiration

A piercing drop engulfs your doubts. They become others burdens. A bind uncertainty molds creativity the monster of colors

A grave of battered minds fill a visible void. Plot the breakdowns of madness. A desperate being searches for an escape the relapse of happiness burdens

It makes us WHOLE, you see?

HOLE

Underselling my shit

Why do we linger with the critics?
Reviews on morals and décor
They never get the adjectives right

Captions like headlines
Did you read between the lines?
I read every word you never jotted down

We clung like quotation marks
Hanging on every word
I was too afraid to speak
So, I wrote

Four stars to the breakdowns needed for
Creation

None of it was necessary
But at least she wrote it well

It's not Perfect or the Right Kind

Who told you to stop running when it fits you so well
Stop waiting for a sign & wash your hands
You don't belong here

He rests his head on my chest
And hugs me like he's diving into the ocean
we sink
when we should float
we crash into the rocks shaping our way

It's the crash that drowns me
The reaching

I used to love it because it wasn't perfect
Or the right kind
but I felt it

But that's just it
It's not perfect
or the right kind
It's just doing everything to be felt

Crumbled

There's crumbs of you stuck in
Between my sheets
I notice them when my feet get cold

When I wallow in covers
Too selfish to share myself with the sun
I bury myself in my roots
There's reassurance in regrowth

I don't like crumbs in my bed
but there's crumbs of you in my sheets
crumbs in a place I never fucking eat

Dog Lovers Know

What it's like before you learn how to bark
How often you find yourself in whimpers
Shuffling about trying to find your voice
Wiggling with uncertainty

When your young there's little reason to bark
Days spent chasing clouds and dreams
It's the fear that summons it
Strikes you like lightning to sand
Hardening the gaps

Forces the sharp sound out
At first, it's frightening
That loudness
That don't forgive me for my volume
But I will be heard rush of adrenaline

Sometimes I miss the innocence of the silence
The time before my bark summoned politics
When I didn't have to bark for precaution

When my volume didn't have to worry
about the dangers of shattering glass ceilings

Truth is

Even if I could go back
I wouldn't belong there anymore
Like the puzzle piece that
Somewhat fits
But not quite

My pointed edges pricking the curves
Of your perfectly painted landscape

Truth is
The growth always
Surpasses the memories
Hold me too tight
My buttons pop right off
We pop right off

Truth is
I never wanted to let you go
I needed to let you go

She who Shall Not be Named

I sit in our drive way
Her car at the curbside
I sit in silence
No tears

It's the middle of summer
& I can feel the frost on my nose
If Lincoln could talk
he'd tell you to watch the house
with the yellow door

I come home with questions
That can't be asked
Because god forbid your ego speak

Wipe your questions at the door
Make dinner for a family that isn't yours
I sit in silence; her car at the curbside

What am I doing here?
But God forbid my ego speak

Brewed

Steep me in uncertainty
Boil the tension
To bring out my natural aroma

Sharp & energetic
I never said I'd be your cup of tea
Steep me in the sleepless nights
Wake up to me

Let's brew together
Pour ourselves as one
Smooth & warm
Filled to the brim

It's the soft morning rituals
That drink me up

WANDER

Wanderers below the treetops
Green grows on my cold brown skin
There are three seeds beneath
My brown soil
You only saw one bloom

Roots

It's always the stirring of the seasoning
that soothes my soul
The recipes we hold in the
Library of our hearts

Mira la olla
Forever burning my tongue
Growing my roots in the kitchen
Seasoning my soul
I stir with an open heart
and pass the seeds of my mothers
down on a plate
My roots simmered for my sun
Mira la olla con todo

Everything Goes up in Smoke

As I stared at the smoke
I marveled at the way it floated
towards the clouds
Fascinated at the magical force
that seemed to hold it together
and tear it apart at the same time
It's funny because I know that
feeling all too well

For them to Catch a Giant

Watching them dig in the sand
How ten years will change them
Will effect them
Who they will be
Become
From digging in the sand
To digging themselves out of the sand
For them to catch a giant

Hold the door open

For the longest time, I felt the calling to write
To smear words on paper and label it art
I moved slowly at first, cautiously
For the longest time, I felt as though
I was moving too slow
The universe was holding the door open for me
And I was taking my time
Losing myself on punctuation
Crossing out sentences
that made cents to the senses
I walk through this door without fear
And I thank you all
For holding the door open for me

Acknowledgements

If anyone knows how much this piece of work has taken out of me,
it's my father.
He's my confidant, my editor, and was my biggest critic on my writing until I made him a fan.
If I learned anything, it was that documentation immortalized things.
You are holding pieces of my life, panic, and joys in your hand.
To the man that pushed me to write, that believed I'd do it since I wrote my first piece.
For every late night, you spent proofing my work to every time I refused to write because I didn't want
to give away my magic.

Thank you,
for seeing me, but more importantly for taking the time to explore my art with me.
It's been a hell of a journey.

www.ingramcontent.com/pod-product-compliance
Lightning Source LLC
Chambersburg PA
CBHW022021290426
44109CB00015B/1266